Not All Is As It Seems

A Collection Of Haikus Bringing Attention
To The Paths We All Are Walking

Ryan Lee Bobillo

India | USA | UK

Made with ❤ on the BookLeaf Publishing Platform
www.bookleafpub.in
www.bookleafpub.com

Dedication

This book of poems is dedicated to whomever reads it. I hope that this helps to bring you awareness, light, love, and whatever you may be needing in the moment. Time is a funny thing, and its something that we all share and lose in the same manner. So, in the same manner that we all lose time inevitably, It is my wish that this book finds your eyes, mind, and heart. Inevitably.

Sending Love & Light,

Ryan Lee Bobillo

Preface

2025 is here...... Is this how you thought it would look? Is this how you thought it would feel? I am certain that if you are taking time to read this collection of haikus, then you may have some strong feelings about the path we, as a collective human race are haphazardly running down. Considering we are only 10% into the year at the time of this Preface being written; the references, themes and connotations in this book may be comically out of date by the time this gets into your hands or illuminates the pixels on your screen. Whether thats because the publishing company is swamped with pushing all manners of paper and PDFs containing millions of words all valued at roughly a penny a petabyte; or possibly this collection was just bookmarked in your favorites and you didn't get around to reading it until you cleaned out your inbox while waiting for your flight home or catching your Uber from work. Regardless, I hope the following helps you to not just consider the time we are living in, but also that you can change your perspective, your course, or your current situation at any time with the right decision and action. With 2025 seemingly being a year of conclusions, I encourage all of you reading to look deep, read between, and always consider that many things nowadays, are not actually at all how they seem.

Acknowledgements

I would like to thank all of my past English writing teachers and professors who collectively helped me to find the magic and enjoyment in reading and writing of all kinds. And thank you to Coffee Cake, you are my lightening in a bottle.

NO AI WAS USED IN THE CREATION OF THESE WRITINGS

1. On Ownership

White Picket Fences

And Cold Steel Bars Sliding Shut

Have the Same Owners

2. Money Matters

Only At the Top

Can you Fuck Up, Up, and Up

And the Bottom Pays

3. Bread & Circus

Chief, Killed by Eagles

Shots Fired, K-Dot, Red Dot

Swiftly, Mahomes Fell Twice

4. Fin Tech

In Water and Coin

Those Floundering and Alone

Always Attract Sharks

5. Mayday

All Things that Fly While

Searching For Signals are Now

Shackled and Metered

6. Snow Moon

New Moons Colder than

Bones, Under Fresh Snowfall, Still

Pull at Empty Hearts

7. Abroad

A World Connected

By Crumbling Dots, Worn Twine

Makes it a Journey

8. Emeralds are Forever

Emerald Tablets

Are Within Each One of Us

Waiting Translation

9. Growing Pains

To Grow, Is to Know

The Broadest Spectrums of Pain,

Loss, and of Setback

10. In War

Know Your Enemies

Get Acquainted in Battles

Unspoken and Not

11. Heart Burns

Hearts Are Truly Blind

Too Focused on Keeping You

Able to Feel Love

12. Empire of Ottomans

Us Here, So Mighty

So Much to Say And Support

But Our Feet Are Up

13. A World Withered

From Green To Grey Scale

A Once Lush World Cries For Help

Everyone Filmed It

14. To The Dreamer

Those Who Seek Control

Often, Know Nothing of Self

You're Always On Sale

15. Exercising Team Spirit

In A World So Tense

Lets Not Crash Out and Throw Hands

Instead, Lets Lend One

16. Stuck Between A Rock And A Hard Life

Vows, Diamonds, A Kiss

All Are Meaningless If You

Forget How To Share

17. Big Eye In The Sky

It Sees All Far Out

And Beyond, Parading Stars

Into The Abyss

18. Scroll Hole

While Soldiers Shoot Mines

Citizens Watch From Above

Drone Kamikazes

19. This Is An Adventure

Being Unprepared

Makes You Live For Uprooting

For Needing A Map

20. A New Age

Shed The Old Ways Now

Unhand Any Dead Weight Now

New Days Run Like Ink

21. Not All Is As It Seems

Despite Perversion

Of Mind and of Hand, D.L.

Achieved Samadhi